PIONEERS
OF CANADA

THE SCHOOLHOUSE

JILL FORAN

Weigl

Published by Weigl Educational Publishers Limited
6325 10th Street SE
Calgary, Alberta
T2H 2Z9

Website: www.weigl.ca

Library and Archives Canada Cataloguing in Publication

Foran, Jill
    The schoolhouse / Jill Foran.

(Pioneers of Canada)
Includes index.
ISBN 978-1-77071-680-3 (bound).--ISBN 978-1-77071-684-1 (pbk.)

    1. Schools--Canada--History--Juvenile literature.
2. Education--Canada--History--Juvenile literature. 3. Frontier and pioneer life--Canada--Juvenile literature. I. Title. II. Series: Pioneers of Canada (Calgary, Alta.)

LA411.F67 2011   j371.00971   C2011-904769-1

Printed in the United States of America in North Mankato, Minnesota
1 2 3 4 5 6 7 8 9 0 15 14 13 12 11

072011
WEP040711

Project Coordinator: Jordan McGill
Design: Terry Paulhus

Photograph Credits
Dreamstime: pages 9, 11; Getty Images: pages 1, 9, 11, 13, 14, 15, 16, 17, 21, 22; Glenbow Museum: pages 1, 5, 6, 7, 10, 12, 18, 19, 20.

Every reasonable effort has been made to trace ownership and to obtain permission to reprint copyright material. The publishers would be pleased to have any errors or omissions brought to their attention so that they may be corrected in subsequent printings.

We acknowledge the financial support of the Government of Canada through the Canada Book Fund for our publishing activities.

CONTENTS

INTRODUCTION

Imagine your life without school or learning. Long ago, children in Canada did not have schools to go to. When **pioneers** first arrived in Canada, there was no time to build schools. The pioneers were too busy building houses, planting **crops**, and finding ways to stay alive in their new country. At first, many pioneer children were taught how to read and write at home. Some children were not taught these skills. Instead, they helped their parents with **chores**. As communities began to grow, schoolhouses were built.

In the early 1800s, if parents wanted a school for their children, they had to build the school themselves. Families in a community gathered together to build the schoolhouse. Once the schoolhouse was constructed, it was up to the community to look after it and keep it in good shape.

THE SCHOOLHOUSE

Canada's early schoolhouses were simple log buildings. They had four walls, a roof, and only one room. All the students learned in this one classroom. Windows let in just enough light for the students to see. The students sat on uncomfortable wooden benches.

teacher had to start
the stove every morning.
the teacher also had
to stack the firewood.

In the early days, the most important piece of furniture in the classroom was the big stove. The stove stood in the middle of the room. It was the school's only source of heat. In the winter, the stove burned all the time. Students would try to huddle up to the stove as often as they could to keep warm.

SCHOOLHOUSE TOOLS

Students in early Canadian schools did not have many supplies. In the 1800s, many schools did not have pencils to write with. There were no computers or library books to use for research. Many schools had no maps. At first, students did not even have notebooks. The school supplies that early students used are very different from those used today.

Slates

In pioneer schools, students used small slate boards. Slates worked like small blackboards. Each student had his or her own slate board and slate chalk. During lessons, students wrote questions and spelling words on their slates. After each lesson, students wiped their slates clean.

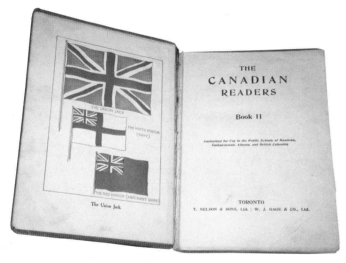

Readers

Canada's early schoolhouses did not have bookshelves full of books. At first, teachers used whatever books they could find. As more time passed, textbooks called readers were published for students. Readers were used for learning how to read and spell.

Quills and Ink

Older students also used pens called quills. Quill pens were long feathers sharpened at the tip. Students dipped the quill's sharp tip into homemade ink. They used the quill to practise their writing. Students usually had to bring paper from home.

Children would be out of bed by 6:00 a.m. They woke up early to help their parents with chores. Boys helped their fathers feed the farm animals. Girls helped their mothers make breakfast.

After breakfast, boys and girls helped pack their lunches in the tin pails they carried to school. Most of the time, lunches included food items such as hardboiled eggs, baked potatoes, bread and butter, and apples.

After lunch was packed, children began the long walk to school. Most students arrived at the schoolhouse by 8:00 a.m. The students gathered outside the school and waited for the teacher to ring the school bell.

THE BELL SOUNDS

When the teacher rang the bell, the students lined up at the schoolhouse door. They stood shortest to tallest, and waited for the teacher to let them in the classroom. After they entered the classroom, they stood by their desks and said good morning to the teacher. **Prayers** or songs followed the greeting.

S ince all grades were together in one room, the teacher was very busy. There were only three subjects, reading, writing, and **arithmetic**. Students did much of their learning by memorizing their lessons.

During the morning, students stopped their lessons for recess. They rushed outside to enjoy 15 minutes of playtime. The teacher rang the school bell at the end of recess. On their way back inside, students would take a drink of water from a dipper that was placed in a pail of water.

After more lessons, it was time for lunch. Students ate quickly, then played games, such as tag and marbles. Some students made trips to the **outhouse**. Early schools did not have indoor bathrooms.

Pioneer students were expected to bring water into the schoolhouse. Some schools had large jars to keep the water cool and clean. Students had to go outside and pump water that came from underground.

After lunch, students looked at their readers. They read aloud to the teacher. Younger students could learn by listening to older students read aloud. Some schools also had school gardens. In those schools, students might spend time in the afternoon working in the school garden. They worked to keep their school garden clean and healthy.

Nisbet School S. D. No 19 Alberta

Standard VI Bessie Johnston   Standard III Ira Trace   Part I
V Mary Latimer   II Guy Trace   I
V Agnes Bookless   Part II Otto Krause
V Dora Sannes   Ernest Krause   Sept. 24. 19

Pioneer teachers wrote the students' lessons on the blackboard at the front of the room. Lessons for each grade were written on a separate part of the blackboard.

At 4:00, school was over for the day. The teacher dismissed the class. One or two students stayed behind to help the teacher sweep and clean the classroom. As children began their long walk home, they thought about the chores and homework they still had to do.

Once home, young boys' chores included feeding **livestock** and gathering firewood. Girls fed the chickens, washed dishes, set the table, and gathered vegetables. As the children aged, they took on more chores. Boys would plow and cut wood. Girls cared for younger children and made clothes.

TEACHERS

Schools in early Canada were very different from schools today. Most schools today have more than one classroom, and many teachers teach at one school. Teachers today have access to new tools, such as computers and interactive whiteboards, to help teach. There are more subjects to teach today. However, teachers still teach reading, writing, and arithmetic, just like at early schools.

THEN AND NOW DIAGRAM

DIAGRAM

There are many differences between today's schools and those of long ago. The diagram on the right compares these differences and similarities. Copy the diagram in your notebook. Try to think of similarities and differences to add to your diagram.

THEN

- Usually, there is only one classroom.
- Children of all ages share the same teacher and classroom.
- Students write with quill pens.
- Students use slate boards.
- Students walk long distances to school.
- A wood stove heats the classroom.
- Windows are the only source of light.

- Students bring their lunches to school.
- Everyone plays games at recess.
- Students help keep their classroom clean.
- Students learn how to read, write, and solve math problems.
- Students use textbooks.

NOW

- There are many classrooms.
- There are different teachers for different grades.
- Students write with pencils and pens.
- Students use computers.
- Classrooms are heated with modern heaters.
- Electric lights provide light in classrooms.
- Students study more than three subjects.

GLOSSARY

arithmetic: mathematics, such as addition, subtraction, division, and multiplication

chores: jobs done around the house and farm

crops: plants that are grown as food

livestock: farm animals kept for a purpose

outhouse: an outdoor toilet with no plumbing

pioneers: a person who is among the first to settle a new country or area

prayers: a request or thanks spoken to a god or object of worship

INDEX